Bob Hart
New Testament Tales

The Unauthorized Version

Now for the other side of the story!

The Bible version of the stories of Jesus is rightly treated as – er, Gospel. But there were plenty of characters on the sidelines who saw things from a different angle.

Packed full of humour, mischief, silliness, and fun: these unauthorized versions from master storyteller Bob Hartman get to the heart of the matter.

Bob Hartman knows how to captivate an audience, and regularly entertains children and adults around the world as a performance storyteller. He is perhaps best known for the widely acclaimed *Lion Storyteller Bible*. When he is not writing, Bob enjoys making music, reading about classic cars, and entertaining his grandchildren.

Text copyright © 2012 Bob Hartman
This edition copyright © 2012 Lion Hudson

The moral rights of the author have been asserted

A Lion Children's Book
an imprint of
Lion Hudson plc
Wilkinson House, Jordan Hill Road,
Oxford OX2 8DR, England
www.lionhudson.com
ISBN 978 0 7459 6284 9 (print)
ISBN 978 0 7459 6728 8 (epub)
ISBN 978 0 7459 6727 1 (Kindle)
ISBN 978 0 7459 6729 5 (PDF)

First edition 2012
10 9 8 7 6 5 4 3 2 1 0
First electronic edition 2012

A catalogue record for this book is available
from the British Library

Typeset in 14/17 Baskerville MT Schoolbook
Printed and bound in Great Britain by Clays Ltd, St Ives plc

Distributed by:
UK: Marston Book Services Ltd, PO Box 269, Abingdon, Oxon
OX14 4YN
USA: Trafalgar Square Publishing, 814 N Franklin Street, Chicago,
IL 60610
USA Christian Market: Kregel Publications, PO Box 2607, Grand Rapids,
MI 49501

Bob Hartman's New Testament Tales

THE UNAUTHORIZED VERSION

LION
CHILDREN'S

Contents

Introduction

Why "Unauthorized"?

Well, in 2011, the Authorized or King James Version of the Bible celebrated its 400th anniversary, and I thought that it might be fun to write an Unauthorized Version.

As "Authorized" suggests "official", "traditional", "approved of", I figured that an unauthorized version of the Bible stories would come from the point of view of sources that were not official or traditional. So I set about making up other voices to tell these familiar stories:

- the boy on the hill who was desperate to swap his lunch of fish and bread
- the brother of the bride at the wedding in Cana
- the dead boy Jesus raised.

I tried to tell the stories in a way that would be true to the original, but also in a way that would bring out the humour in them.

I sort of doubt that anyone will be reading these in 400 years' time, but I hope that you enjoy them, and that you chuckle (at least a little). That will be approval enough for me.

Bob Hartman

The Landlord's Version

The Shepherds and the Birth of Jesus

"Watch where you're stepping!" Avi's mum shouted as he sleepily slipped down the stairs.

"What?" the boy grunted. And then, "Why?"

"Ask your father," she grunted back. "And then maybe, once he's answered you, he'll get off his backside and give me a hand."

Avi's dad tipped his stool, leaned back against the wall, and grinned. "It was nothing, Son. Just a little party we had here last night."

"A little party?" said Avi's mum. "That's how you describe it?" Her voice was getting louder.

"A LITTLE PARTY?" And now she was shouting.

"OK, a right old knees-up!" he admitted.

"With…?" she added.

"With a load of shepherds," he smiled.

Avi scratched his head. "Shepherds? I didn't know you knew any shepherds."

"We most certainly do not know any shepherds!" Avi's mum grumbled. "Nobody in polite society knows any shepherds." She was glaring at his dad now. "NOBODY!"

"To be fair," he corrected her, "we actually do know some shepherds now. There was old Samuel. And young Elijah. And that little man with the crusty thing wrapped around his foot…"

"That WAS his foot!" Avi's mum muttered darkly. "And don't put that thing in your mouth!" she shouted at Avi's little sister, Hanna, who was sitting on the floor.

"Marble," said Hanna.

And Avi's mum stomped across the room and snatched it from her two-year-old fingers.

"Do you see what you have done?" she cried, waving the thing that was not a marble at Avi's dad.

"Calm down, dear," he shrugged. "A little sheep poo

7

never hurt anyone. Although," he continued, looking closer, "that might actually BE a marble."

Avi's mum stamped her foot. "I will not calm down. We are a respectable inn. Never in my wildest dreams did I imagine that I would be sweeping up after sheep in this dining room!"

"So how did the shepherds get here in the first place?" Avi asked.

"An excellent question!" Avi's mum replied. She was glaring at his dad again. "Shall I answer, darling, or would you like to?"

"They were happy," said Avi's dad. "They were running up and down the street, shouting about the good news that they wanted to share."

"That doesn't sound so bad," Avi shrugged.

"Really?" his mother sneered, digging a clump of wool out of Hanna's cheek. "Not so bad? Then why did Martha up at the Rook and Rock Badger slam the door on them? Why did Melchizedek blow out every lamp at the Hoof and Hippo?"

"Because they didn't want to hear the news?" guessed Avi.

"Because they were SHEPHERDS!" she shouted. "Filthy, stinking, flea-bitten, sheep-shifting shepherds! And nobody with any concern for their reputation," she was glaring at Avi's dad yet again, "lets a gang of shepherds into their establishment!"

"So what was the good news?" asked Avi, sheepishly.

"Craziness," grumbled his mum.

"Now that's a matter of opinion, dear," said his dad. "It seems that the shepherds had – how shall I put it – a run-in with some angels."

"Angels?" said Avi. "That does actually sound kind of crazy."

But Avi's dad wasn't giving up. "I'll admit it,"

he said. "It all sounded a little crazy to me, too. But I had a good sniff at them and none of them had even a hint of alcohol on their breath. They were sober. And I should know."

"So they met these angels…" said Avi. "And then…?"

"And then the angels told them something about the messiah," his dad went on.

"The messiah?" Avi asked.

"With the emphasis on mess," his mother sighed. "I'll never get this place clean! Hanna, do not stick that up your nose!"

"Yes, the messiah," his dad answered. "The special saviour that God promised to send our people to deliver us from our enemies."

"What did they say?" asked Avi.

"The angels told the shepherds that the messiah had been born. Here in Bethlehem. Last night. At an inn up the road."

Avi's mother rolled her eyes. "The Dog and Donkey, of all places. Biggest dump in town. As if God would let the messiah be born there!"

"Well, that's what the angels said," his dad continued. "And that's where the shepherds went after the angels sang a song."

"A song?" said Avi.

"Yeah. Something about peace on earth and goodwill to men. The shepherds sang it for me. It was catchy."

"It was crazy!" Avi's mum countered. "Songs blaring. Sheep bleating. Not one of them in tune!"

"What, the sheep?" asked Avi.

"No, the shepherds!" shouted his mum. "I'm surprised you got any sleep at all."

"The boy was probably counting sheep," joked Avi's dad. But his mum was not smiling.

"Sorry," he muttered. "Anyway, the shepherds said that they went up to the inn and, sure enough, there in the cowshed – out the back – they found a man and a woman and a newborn baby."

"And the baby was lying where?" Avi's mother huffed. "Go on, tell him."

"In the feed trough," said Avi's dad.

"The feed trough?" said Avi. "Really?"

"Really!" nodded his mum. "So these shepherds said. Now you tell me – what kind of god sends his special long-awaited saviour to earth and gives him to a family who sticks him, not one day old, in a feed trough?"

"The angels said it was a sign," his dad protested, "so that the shepherds would know they were at the right place."

"Furthermore," his mum went on, "what kind of god sends this special long-awaited saviour to be born in the back of a run-down inn, while there are at least three respectable establishments in the same town from which to choose?"

"Now, dear," said Avi's dad, "there's no need to take this personally."

"And finally," she said finally, "what kind of god sends an angelic choir to announce the birth of his long-awaited saviour to a filthy, flea-infested bunch of tone deaf shepherds? Hanna, I will not say it again, take that out of your mouth!"

"More marble," said Hanna.

"I'll tell you what kind of god!" she shouted. "A god for crazy people. Crazy unwashed people who have spent far too many lonely nights on the hills outside this city!"

Then she crossed her arms and stamped one foot and waited for a response.

"D'you want to go up to the Dog and Donkey to have a look?" said Avi.

"I was hoping you'd ask," grinned his dad.

"And now you have both gone crazy, too," sighed his mum. "Well, if you must go, why don't you take your sister with you? She's already had her daily ration of sheep poo. A nap in a feed trough would probably suit her just right!"

"OK, Mum," Avi chuckled as he disappeared out of the door.

"We'll be right back," said his dad, scooping up Hanna. "We won't be long. And when we get back," he added, "we'll help you clean up this place. Promise."

Avi's mum rolled her eyes. "Now that really would be good news."

The Brother's Version

The Wedding at Cana

Gehazi's Aunt Miriam grabbed his face with her two pudgy hands and placed her equally pudgy lips on his forehead. "Your sister is such a beautiful bride!" she beamed. "You should be proud. And what a handsome young man you are!"

The kiss left two fat wet spots. It was all he could do to keep himself from wiping them away.

"Thanks, Aunt," he said with as much enthusiasm as he could muster. Which wasn't much enthusiasm, to be honest, seeing as she was probably the twentieth aunt who had done much the same thing.

And then one of the servants asked her if she wanted some wine. And she said, "Yes, of course, how delightful." And Gehazi was mercifully left on his own again.

Weddings. For a boy with five big sisters and only two of them already married, weddings were torture. Torture then. Torture now. Torture yet to come.

The only thing that made this particular wedding bearable was that Anna, the bride, was his favourite sister and Adam, the bridegroom, was just about the nicest guy he'd ever met.

His other sisters' husbands hardly knew he existed. But Adam treated him almost as if he was one of his own brothers. Which meant a lot to a boy who had no brothers of his own.

So Gehazi stood there and smiled and put up with the kisses and the head-patting and the relatives who couldn't even remember his name.

"Psst," came a whisper from the other side of the doorway. "Over here." And then there was his cousin, Shem.

"Go away," Gehazi whispered back. "I'm busy. I don't want to get in trouble."

Shem crept through the doorway. The whisper got louder. "Who said anything about getting into trouble?"

Gehazi rolled his eyes. "You're here. There will be trouble. There always is."

Shem sniggered. "Yeah, but you've got to admit it – I always have fun. Like when I set the donkey loose at MY sister's wedding."

Gehazi grinned. "Yes, it was pretty good when it wandered into the reception and knocked over the pudding."

"On Uncle Ezra!" Shem chuckled. "Classic!"

"But you hate your sister," Gehazi reminded him.

"Hate?" Shem chuckled again. "No, I don't!

I just think she's stuck-up and knows it all and is her daddy's little princess and looks like a pig. But I don't hate her."

"Well, I like my sister," said Gehazi. "And I don't want to spoil her wedding. So no trouble, OK?"

"No trouble," Shem shrugged. "But that doesn't mean that we can't sneak out the back for a while and find something more interesting to do."

"I don't know…" Gehazi hesitated. And then another aunt – Aunt Agatha – grabbed his face.

Gehazi held his breath. Shem cringed.

And when another fat slobbery kiss had ended, Aunt Agatha looked at Shem and shook her finger in his direction. "Don't think YOU'LL be getting one of those," she grunted. "Not after that prank you played at your uncle's funeral."

Then she stamped away. And Gehazi exhaled at last.

"Terrible breath," noted Shem.

"Like a rotting corpse," agreed Gehazi. "So what happened at the funeral?"

Shem smiled. "You remember that little high pitched sneezy sound that Uncle Judah used to make? Well, at the funeral, I hid behind the coffin, and when Aunt Death-Breath walked by, I sort of did an impersonation of it."

"And…" asked Gehazi.

"And she nearly died, too," Shem grinned. "I can't

help it if people don't have a sense of humour."

"That's what I mean," Gehazi sighed. "You think 'funny'. Everybody else thinks 'trouble'."

"Oh, c'mon," Shem pleaded. "Look, Aunt Hilda is coming this way. She's got that thing on her face. That thing that looks like a camel. You don't really want that thing touching you, do you?"

"Point taken," Gehazi nodded. And the two of them took off in the direction of the kitchen.

"Not much going on back here," observed Gehazi as several servants scurried past them.

"Not much that's interesting anyway," Shem sighed. And then he peeped around the corner into a storage area and his eyes lit up. "You have got to see this melon!" he grinned.

"There are plenty of melons out there on the tables," said Gehazi, looking around. He was starting to get a little nervous.

"Not like this melon," said Shem, steering his cousin around the corner and pointing up to a shelf. "LOOK!"

So Gehazi looked. And when he did, he couldn't help but laugh.

"It's amazing, isn't it?" laughed Shem as well. "Looks just like the head of our dear departed Uncle Judah! I'm going to climb up there and grab that melon – and set it on Aunt Death-Breath's table when she isn't looking."

"I don't know…" Gehazi hesitated. "I told you I don't want to spoil the wedding."

"It won't spoil anything!" Shem argued. "Come on, give me a boost."

Gehazi was still hesitant. "I just think that maybe…"

"All right then," grunted Shem. "I'll do it myself." And he stepped up onto the edge of a tall jar of wine.

"Careful," warned Gehazi.

"I'll be fine," Shem smiled, reaching for the melon.

But as he grabbed the melon, he lost his balance. And the jar tipped. And as it fell, it tipped into another jar. Which tipped into another. And by the time Shem hit the floor, it was covered in wine.

"I did not expect that," said Shem, clutching the melon. "Oh, and I think I hear my mum calling. See you, Cuz."

And he dashed out of the storage area, leaving Gehazi alone with a pile of broken jars and a pool of wine.

He wasn't alone for long, though.

A servant rounded the corner and when he saw the mess, he cried, "What have you done?"

"Nothing," Gehazi pleaded. "Nothing. It wasn't me!"

"Well, it was somebody," said the servant. "And you're the only one standing there. The last time I left this room, it was filled with wine. And now… you have somehow managed to break every jar! This is all we had!"

"But it wasn't me!" Gehazi said again. And then he realized. It didn't really matter. The wine was gone. That was what mattered. And his sister's wedding was ruined!

Another minute and another head popped around

the corner. Gehazi cringed. Of all the people in the wedding, it had to be… Aunt Agatha.

"WHAT is going on in here?" she demanded. And Gehazi and the servant both started talking at once.

Aunt Agatha held up one hand to silence them. She looked at the mess and at the boy and at the servant. Then she looked especially hard at the small purple footprints exiting the room.

"There is no need to explain," she said. "You," she continued, pointing at the servant, "need to clean this place up. And you," she went on, looking straight at Gehazi, "need to be careful of the company you keep."

Just then, one more head peeped around the corner.

"Mary, my dear," Aunt Agatha sighed, "there appears to have been a bit of an… accident back here. It seems we've run out of wine."

"And now my sister's wedding is ruined!" added Gehazi, wiping one eye with the back of his hand.

Mary looked around the room. Then she put a hand on Aunt Agatha's shoulder. "I just might be able to help," she said calmly. "Or rather, my son might. I'll have a word with him. Leave it to me." And she slipped away.

"Who was that?" asked Gehazi.

"An old friend. From Nazareth," said Aunt Agatha. "She's here with her son, Jesus."

"Does he sell wine?" Gehazi wondered out loud.

"No," answered his aunt. "He's a rabbi. Can't imagine how he could help. Bit of a mystery, actually. But then, I like a good mystery!" And her eyes twinkled mischievously. "Now let's get you cleaned up."

When they emerged from the storage room, the servant had not yet returned to clear up the mess.

And when Aunt Agatha saw him chatting excitedly with all the other servants, she shouted, "I thought I told you to clean up that room!"

"Sorry. Very sorry," the servant apologized. "I was on my way to do it. And then another lady stopped me and told me to go and talk to her son. She said that he would be able to find us some more wine."

"That must have been your friend," said Gehazi to his aunt.

"Exactly what I was thinking," she nodded. The twinkle was back in her eye. "And what did he tell you?" she asked the servant.

"The man said that we should pour water into these six stone jars."

"Very curious," said Aunt Agatha. "And…?"

"So we did," answered the servant.

"And…?" said Aunt Agatha again.

"And you can taste it for yourself!" said another servant, dipping a cup into the jar and handing it to her.

Aunt Agatha took a sip from the cup and her eyes popped wide open.

"What is it?" asked Gehazi.

"It's wine! And not just any wine, but probably the best I've ever tasted."

"But how?" asked Gehazi. "How did Jesus do it?"

"Who knows?" said Aunt Agatha. "And who cares? Your sister's wedding has been saved. That's all that matters." Then she dipped her cup back into the jar and had another drink. "And you boys had better start passing this around before I finish it all."

Gehazi watched as the wine went around the

room – and as each and every guest reacted as his aunt had. He went over to talk to his sister and her husband, but was stopped by the master of the banquet. To Gehazi's surprise, the man started shaking his new brother-in-law by the hand.

"Sir," the man said, "most hosts serve their best wine first, but you have saved the best until last!"

And then Gehazi heard a scream from the other side of the hall.

"Oh no!" he thought. "I forgot to warn Aunt Agatha about the Uncle Judah Melon Head."

He raced across the room, and that's when he saw it. The scream had not come from Aunt Agatha at all. It had come from his cousin Shem. His aunt had a tight grip on the boy's ear and was dragging him toward the storage room.

"Please, Aunt, let go!" he pleaded. "It was only a bit of fun."

"And I have a bit of fun for you!" she answered. "Helping to clear up the mess you made."

"Cuz! Cuz!" he called to Gehazi. "Give me a hand here!"

"Sorry," Gehazi grinned, "got to go. I think I hear my mum calling."

Sonny's Version

Jesus and the Sons of Zebedee

Abraham ben Abraham hated cats.

This was not unusual for his time. In the first century in Galilee, which was when and where Abraham ben Abraham lived, everybody hated cats.

They didn't curl up on people's cushions. They didn't get fed from brightly coloured bowls. And nobody kept them as pets.

They got ignored. Or shouted at. Or kicked across the street. And that was by people who simply didn't like them. Not by people like Abraham ben Abraham who despised their very existence.

The reason that Abraham ben Abraham hated cats, along with his father, and his father's father (who were all called Abraham ben Abraham), is that he was a fisherman. And for a fisherman, fish equals profit. The more fish, the more profit. The fewer fish, the less profit.

And because cats eat fish and have no qualms about pinching them from the nets of hard-working fishermen, fish plus cat equals less profit. So Abraham ben Abraham hated cats.

Abraham ben Abraham had a son. A son called Sonny. It was officially, of course, Abraham ben Abraham. But because "ben" means "son of", Sonny thought that "Sonny" would make a nice nickname – and that it would also annoy his father.

Annoying his father was not Sonny's only goal in life, but it was at the top of the list. At position number one, actually. He was eleven – nearly a man by the standards of his day – and determined not to be ruled by his father's expectations. It will therefore come as no surprise that the number two goal in Sonny's life was to have a cat.

A particular cat, as it happens. A scruffy, thin, ginger cat with a tail shaped like a question mark. A cat called Pat.

Sonny did not know this was the cat's name, of course, because in first-century Galilee, nobody called cats names. Well, they did. They called them names like "Getlost" or "Goaway" or "Thievinglittleswine".

Which is why the cats came up with names of their own. Nicer names, on the whole. Names like "Tickle". Or "Scratch". Or "Pat".

And so it was that one foggy morning, Abraham ben Abraham and Sonny and Pat the cat made their way, each in his own way, to a fishing boat, moored at the Sea of Galilee.

Abraham ben Abraham's "way" could be described as "completely cheesed off with the world". On this particular morning, Abraham ben Abraham was completely cheesed off with his chief competitors – a pair of brothers called James and John ben Zebedee.

"Flippin' unfair advantage," he muttered.
"Blinkin' luck," he grumbled.

Sonny had heard it all before and had managed to work out that it had to do with the brothers sharing a rather nice boat with their father – the "Zebedee" bit of "ben Zebedee".

He couldn't have cared less, as it happens, which was his "way". And he managed to look as uninterested as possible whenever his father's rants grew loudest. Which annoyed Abraham ben Abraham no end (see Sonny's number one goal).

Pat's "way" was to sniff around fishing boats, which was what he was doing as Abraham ben Abraham and Sonny arrived.

"Getlost… youthievinglittleswine!" shouted Abraham ben Abraham, using what the cat assumed were the man's first and last names for him. So he did, straightening his tail into an exclamation mark and scampering away.

Abraham ben Abraham climbed into the boat and set about doing a variety of "setting out to sea" tasks.

Sonny wasn't much interested in such things. But seeing as his survival depended on knowing what to do in a boat, he forced himself to pay attention.

There was some business

about the mast. And the sail. And the oars. And the nets. Which were inevitably tangled. So it fell to him to untangle them. Which gave him the opportunity to drag them off the boat and onto the shore. Which meant that he could look for Pat.

This, as it turned out, was not difficult. Not nearly as difficult as straightening out a tangled net, at any rate.

Pat was hiding under the edge of the boat. And when Sonny reached into the bag that he carried around his neck and produced a fish head, Pat's tail and whiskers and taste buds rose to attention.

So Sonny laid the fish head beside the net he was straightening. Abraham ben Abraham carried on with his set of seafaring tasks. Pat the cat matched the question mark in his head to the question mark shape that was now his tail and slowly crept out from under the boat toward the tasty fishy treat. And everyone else launched their boats into the sea and set sail. And that included James and John, the sons of Zebedee.

"Blast!" shouted Abraham ben Abraham when he caught sight of the brothers' boat. Then he shouted again. "Where's that flippin' net?"

"Right here!" Sonny shouted back, dragging it in its newly untangled state onto the boat.

"They've got a head start!" he fumed. "Let's get a move on!"

So they did. All that morning and into the early part of the afternoon. And what did they catch?

"Nothing!" grumbled Abraham ben Abraham. "Not a flipper, not a fin, not a…."

"Fing!" added Sonny, trying to sound just that little bit "street" – a habit which annoyed his father nearly as much as sons of Zebedee and cats.

And, speaking of cats, what had happened to Pat?

The answer is quite simple. While everyone else was preparing their boats, Sonny managed to lure the cat closer and closer to him by producing more and more fish heads. And eventually, he managed to lure the cat into the bag itself, where an even greater quantity of fish heads resided. I say "resided". I actually mean "lay there, dead and disjointed from their bodies".

So the cat was literally in the bag. On board the boat. Chewing on fish heads.

I know this seems improbable. All I can say

is that it was a reasonably large bag. And an unusually small cat. And that the fish heads were incredibly delicious. So Pat was willing to "go along for the ride", so to speak – and did, in fact, end up going along for the ride.

As it happens, the ride came to an abrupt end, within shouting distance of the sons of Zebedee.

Shouting was what Abraham ben Abraham was inclined to do whenever he was near the brothers Zebedee. But he was concerned that shouting on this occasion would give rise to the inevitable fisherman's question, "Caught anything yet?"

And since the answer to that question had already been established as "not a flipper, not a fin, not a fing", he didn't want to embarrass himself in front of his chief competitors.

He needn't have worried. James and John had no such qualms. They had never thought of Abraham ben Abraham as their chief competitor. In fact, they barely knew he existed.

This would have brought no comfort to Abraham ben

Abraham. What did bring him comfort, though, was when they shouted back, "No luck today, mate. Haven't caught a thing."

At that point, something unusual happened. Abraham ben Abraham smiled.

And Sonny? Sonny was shocked. For that was the very first time he had ever seen a smile on his father's face.

The fact that it was not a nice smile made little difference to the boy. The fact that the smile had arisen from the complete failure of two fellow fishermen to provide for their families that day was of little concern. Sonny had seen his father smile. In fact, so struck was he by the moment that he very nearly told Abraham ben Abraham about the cat.

But just as he opened his mouth, another unusual thing happened.

Jesus arrived in a boat with Simon, a friend of James and John. He told Simon where to cast his net. Simon did so and hauled in a great catch of fish. Then he called for the sons of Zebedee to help him drag it in, for it was too much for just one boat!

And just as quickly as it had arrived, the smile disappeared from Abraham ben Abraham's face.

Sonny watched it all, amazed. And so he said, quite understandably, "That's unbelievable! That's incredible! That's a miracle!"

Which, in fact, it was.

A point that was not lost on Abraham ben Abraham. "Flippin' sons of Zebedee!" he muttered. "Blinkin' divine intervention!" he moaned.

And, cursing and grumbling, he set sail for home.

Sonny kept his mouth shut all the way. But the cat, unaware of anything but the delights of fish heads, began to purr. The sound of that purr was masked by the washing of the waves against the boat. Until, that is, the vessel bumped with a thump against the shore. And the bag rolled forward. And the purr turned into a noisy meow.

"That's a cat!" shouted Abraham ben Abraham. "A cat in your bag. On my boat!"

And before Sonny could move, his father grabbed the boy's arm with one hand, snatched the bag off the deck with the other, and held it in the air.

Pat the cat squirmed and twisted and yowled.

Sonny begged and pleaded.

"It's been an awful day," sneered Abraham ben Abraham. "But now, at least, there is one thing that will make me happy." And he dangled the bag over the water and laughed the nastiest of nasty cat-drowning laughs.

And then a third unusual thing happened.

James and John and Simon and his brother
Andrew all came walking by.

"We're done with fishing," they announced.
"We're following Jesus now."

"And you, you holding that bag!" shouted John.
"Why don't you have our catch for the day?"

Abraham ben Abraham turned and walked to the end of the boat, letting go of Sonny's arm and dropping the bag on the deck as he went.

"What… what did you say?" he stammered.

"You can have our fish," said John. "They're all yours, mate."

And suddenly the smile was back. And fish, like numbers – indeed, fish-shaped numbers – added themselves up in Abraham ben Abraham's brain. Fish upon fish upon fish upon fish upon profit!

"Did you hear that, boy?" he shouted. "It IS a miracle! A miracle after all!"

And, forgetting everything else, including the cat, he raced off to count his fish.

But Sonny sat down and opened up the bag. He would not have been surprised if the cat was dead. He would not have been surprised if the cat had bolted. He was surprised, however, when somewhat miraculously the cat crept slowly out of the bag and rubbed itself up against his leg.

So he did what you do when a cat does that.

He reached out his hand. And gave him a pat.

The Apprentice's Version

Jesus Heals a Man Lowered Through a Roof

Uncle Saul looked down through the hole and shook his bald head. "Lotta damage here," he grunted. And he sucked a big breath in through his teeth. "Big job. Big, big job. This is gonna cost you."

The man who owned the house looked up through the hole and shook his head as well. "I was afraid of that," he sighed. "Well, it's got to be done. So get on with it – as quick as you can."

And he trudged out of the house and down the street.

"As quick as you can. Right," muttered Uncle Saul.

"Like I've got nothing else to do."

"But you don't, Uncle Saul," I said. "You were telling me just yesterday that the work had dried up."

"That was yesterday!" he snapped. "Today. Today there are deals in the works. Opportunities to be taken advantage of. You've got a lot to learn about business, boy!"

I did, I guess. I was just his apprentice, after all. Tagging along to learn the trade. But I was still confused. Unless Uncle Saul had somehow managed to do a deal in his sleep, I couldn't see how anything had changed from the night before.

"What I want to know," he grumbled, searching through his bag for a measuring line, "is how this happened in the first place."

"I know," I offered. "My friend Andrew told me. Some men did it."

"Men? What, like robbers?" he asked. "It's not the quietest way to break into a place."

"No, no, not robbers," I said. "Just four men."

"Vandals then?" he grunted. "I hate vandals. I say hate… I mean, they're good for business – don't get me wrong. But to tear somebody's roof up just out of spite – that's sick." Then he handed me the end of the line and added, "Hold this. Don't let go."

"I don't think they were vandals either," I said, wrapping the end of the line around my finger, so it wouldn't slip. "But they did have a sick friend."

Uncle Saul paused. "Wait. Wait," he said. "You're telling me that these four guys came up here to vandalize this roof and that they brought their sick friend along just for the fun of it. Now that really is sick!"

"They weren't vandals," I sighed. "That's what YOU said. They were just trying to get their friend into the house."

"And the front door was too much trouble?" he grumbled.

"The front door was blocked," I replied.

"Oh? So if Mr Get-It-Done-Yesterday had simply hired me to fix his door in the first place, he wouldn't be looking at a big bill today. Typical!"

"It wasn't blocked because it was broken," I sighed. "It was blocked because the house was full of people!"

"Sick people?"

"Some of them, yeah, I guess. They were here to see Jesus."

"Jesus the one-eyed spear-sharpener?" he exclaimed. "What did they want to see him for?"

"No, a different Jesus. Jesus the rabbi," I replied.

"Never heard of him," he grunted, letting go of the line. "I think we've got enough tiles to do the job."

"Well, he's kind of famous," I explained.

"Don't have time for celebrities," Uncle Saul shrugged. "I'm a plain, ordinary businessman just trying to make a living. And you'll do well to do the same."

"That's fine," I said. "I'm just saying that he's the reason the four men brought their sick friend along. Because he heals people."

Uncle Saul set a pile of tiles down beside the hole and looked at me very seriously.

"Now, you listen to me, boy. There are lots of folks wandering about, claiming lots of things. They'll tell your future. They'll make it rain. They'll resuscitate your dead donkey. In my experience, most of them are crooks. If you want to make an honest living, stick to construction." And he pounded his fist so hard on the roof that one of the tiles fell through the hole and shattered on the floor below.

"Never mind," he shrugged. "We'll charge him for that one, too. You have to allow for a certain amount of breakage."

"I don't think Jesus is a crook," I answered. "Andrew didn't say anything about his asking for money."

"Oh no," Uncle Saul sneered. "But he doesn't mind encouraging the odd bit of roof-wrecking."

"I don't think he encouraged them to do it. They were just really desperate to get their friend healed."

"So they decided to drop him through a hole in the roof?" Uncle Saul sniggered. "Bet that made him feel better."

"They didn't drop him," I said. "They lowered him on a mat – with ropes tied to the four corners. At least that's what Andrew told me."

"And he knows this how?" asked Uncle Saul, all sceptical.

"Because he was in the room down there," I pointed.

Uncle Saul fitted the tiles together and slowly started to cover up the hole.

"So they lowered him into the room – and then what?"

"People got out of the way. And Jesus talked to him – and that's when the really strange thing happened."

"Oh, like tearing up a roof and lowering a sick guy into a crowded room isn't strange enough?" he grunted.

"Not as strange as this," I said. "Jesus looked at

the man and told him, 'Your sins are forgiven.'"

Uncle Saul dropped another tile. "What did I tell you?" he shouted. "Religious wackos. If it's not money, it's power they're after. So this guy thinks he's God, does he? 'Cause only God can forgive sins."

"That's exactly what the priests said!" I replied. "Some of them were in the house and Andrew said that they were really angry."

"So they set this Jesus straight, did they?"

"Not exactly. No. Before they could do anything, Jesus asked this really weird question: 'Which is easier – to forgive a man's sins or to heal him so he can walk again?'"

"Neither of them's easy!" Uncle Saul snorted. "What kind of question is that?"

"A question Jesus answered himself," I said. "'To prove that I have the power and the right to do the one,' he argued, 'I'll do the other.'

"And he told the man on the mat to get up and walk."

"And…?" asked my uncle Saul, as if he was waiting for the punchline.

"And the man got up and walked!" I said.

Uncle Saul shook his head, as if he was going to take some convincing. "But it still could have been a set-up. The four guys. The sick man. Maybe they were all working for this Jesus character."

And that's when I shook my head. "Don't think so," I said. "The man on the mat – the one who couldn't walk – that was Andrew's dad."

Uncle Saul grunted, "Humph." He was good at grunting. Then he put the last tile in place, and the job was done.

"Don't you think that's amazing?" I asked. "It's like a miracle!"

"What's amazing," he grunted again as he put away his tools, "is that we got this job done so quickly. And as for miracles, I'm just a plain ordinary businessman, trying to make a living. Now pick up that toolbox and let's get going.

There are deals to be made. That's what you need to concentrate on, boy – not all this religious stuff."

So I picked up the toolbox and followed him down off the roof. But I have to admit that I wasn't so sure about what he said – and I wondered, just for a minute, if Jesus could use an apprentice.

The Dead Boy's Version

Jesus Raises the Widow's Son

People always ask me two things: what was it like to die? And what was it like to come back to life again?

The first question is harder, in a way, because I didn't think I was going to die. I was ill. I had a fever. The shakes. That sort of thing. Don't even know where it came from really. It just happened. So I didn't really have any time to think about it.

I guess if I had, I might have been worried or afraid, or I might have thought about how unfair it was to die when I was only thirteen.

But I don't remember thinking any of those things.

I was hot and shaky, then I sort of fell asleep, and that was it. I just didn't wake up again.

I know how my mum felt. At least I know what she told me. She was the one who was worried. Mainly because my dad had died of a fever and she had seen the symptoms before. She didn't say anything, of course, because she didn't want to scare me. But she was scared. Really scared.

And she was the one who thought it was unfair. She'd already lost her husband, and now it looked as if she might lose her son. So she had a word with God. That's what she told me. And she explained to him how wrong she thought it would be.

I died, of course. And she said she that she wasn't just sad. She was angry, too. Angry at God for not making me well. And she was even angry at the friends and relatives who came to pay their respects – angry that they still had sons and husbands to bring with them.

I don't think she said anything to them. I mean, they've never said anything to me about that. But she was angry, I know that.

I think she was also angry that she didn't have any money to pay for the funeral and that she had to rely on those same friends and relatives to help her out. You'd think she would have been pleased that they were there for her. But I think it was a pride thing. Without a husband, she was already poor.

And without a son, well, she would pretty much have to depend on charity for the rest of her life. It's not how you plan for things to work out, is it?

Anyway, there she was in the funeral procession – angry and sad and poor and hopeless, all at the same time. And I was there, too – obviously – bouncing around in my open coffin as my uncles and cousins carried me to my grave. There was a huge crowd – I guess they felt really sorry for my mum. And then all of a sudden, this rabbi called Jesus appeared out of nowhere, walked up to my mum, and said, "Don't cry."

Now, I don't know about you, but I don't think that's the first thing I would say to someone at a funeral. Particularly a total stranger. I think I would say something like "I'm sorry" or "What a shame", or maybe I'd just say nothing at all. But "Don't cry"? Don't be ridiculous!

That's exactly how my mum felt. At least that's what she told me. She didn't know whether to ignore him or spit at him or laugh at him. Or maybe just cry even harder. What she felt like doing was smacking him right across his rabbi face. But instead, she just looked down at the ground and said nothing.

You think that would have stopped the rabbi – dropped the hint that she didn't really want him there; that his comment wasn't exactly right for the occasion.

But no, he just kept going. He walked right up to my coffin and put his hand on it, as if he wanted the procession to stop.

Well, it stopped all right, mainly because everyone was so offended by what he'd done. I mean, what right did he have to burst into a funeral and disrupt everything? My mum told me that there was a lot

of moaning and muttering at that moment. A bit
of shouting and swearing, too. And apparently,
someone had to grab hold of Aaron, our next-door
neighbour, to keep him from doing what my mum
had only thought of doing – and more.

So the funeral was just about wrecked. And that's
when I more or less came back into the picture.

You know how it is when you're really, really

tired, and you fall asleep, and you sleep so soundly that the next thing you know, it's morning and you're awake again? As if no time at all has passed?

Well, that's how it was. Out of nowhere, I heard these words: "Young man, I say to you: get up!"

So I did. And seeing as I didn't actually realize that I was dead, it did sort of feel just like I was getting up. Nothing special. Nothing unusual.

I just opened my eyes and sat up.

Which was, of course, extremely unusual for the people who were attending the funeral!

The swearing turned to swooning. The shouting turned to screaming. And our neighbour Aaron dropped his fists and then fainted and dropped to the ground. It's safe to say that no one in Nain had ever seen anything like this before.

I was obviously shocked as well. What was I doing in a coffin? That was the first thing I wanted to know. But when my mum grabbed me and hugged me and started kissing me and telling me how glad she was to have me back, it became apparent that I had missed a pretty significant event in my life (so to speak).

She hugged Jesus as well, of course, and had plenty to say to him after that – how grateful she was, how amazed she was, how relieved she was, how good it was of God to finally answer her prayers. That sort of thing.

I got a lot of other hugs, too. Well, eventually. Lots of folks were just a little hesitant about putting their arms around someone who had been a corpse just a few minutes earlier. But they got over it, I guess, and in the end, I stepped out of my coffin and walked away from my funeral. And there aren't many people who can say that.

Sad to say, my mum passed away a couple of days ago. We talked a lot before she died and everything was good. She was so happy and so glad that I could be there to hold her hand. So grateful that she wasn't alone. I asked her if she wanted me to try to find Jesus for her, but she said, "No, one person raised from the dead is probably more than any family should expect. And if it had to be anyone," she said, "I'm glad that it was you."

So I'm off to the funeral now. I'm sad. But I'm also sort of glad, in a way. Not just that Jesus brought me back to life, but that, in another way, he brought her back to life, too. I'm not really expecting him to turn up, but who knows? I think I'll keep an eye out for strangers, just in case.

Hector's Version

Jairus' Daughter

I didn't even want the grapes. I just wanted to annoy Gad the Grump.

I wanted to see his red grumpy face and watch him shake his grumpy fist. So I waited for a second, waving the grapes in the air. And when he finally squeezed himself out from behind his market stall, that's when I bolted.

There's this old Greek story about a tortoise and a hare. And I was the hare, zipping between piles of robes and tables of pottery and cartloads of vegetables.

I stopped every now and then, just to see how far he'd come. But I knew the story and I wasn't going to end up short of the finish line. So I gave myself plenty of time to get back to our stall, tossing the grapes to some kids along the way.

And then I waited. Honestly, a tortoise would have been faster. And when he finally arrived, I was quietly rearranging our merchandise, as if I had been there all along.

"You stole… my… grapes," he huffed. "You… little… thief!"

"Don't know what you're talking about, Grump," I shrugged.

"You know… very… well," he puffed. "And… don't call… me that!"

"And why not?" asked Uncle Zeno, his hand suddenly on my shoulder. "You're the grumpiest market trader this side of Jerusalem."

(Which was particularly funny, seeing as Uncle Zeno was not exactly not grumpy.)

"And you're a worthless Greek," grunted Gad. "I don't even know why they let you set up your stall here."

"Because everyone loves a good deal," my uncle grinned. "Jews and Greeks alike. Not the rubbish you peddle."

"Well, it was good enough to steal," the Grump growled.

"I don't see any grapes," my uncle replied. "So why don't you waddle back to your stall and leave the boy alone?"

"May the Lord God curse you and your boy," Gad grunted as he turned to leave.

"Oooh, I'm quaking in my sandals!" mocked Uncle Zeno.

"Cursed by a god nobody has ever seen, with a name nobody is allowed to say."

Then he turned as well – and smacked me on the head.

"What was that for?" I moaned.

"For stealing grapes," he muttered. Then he grinned. "And for not saving any for me."

Xerxes chuckled. He was Uncle Zeno's slave.

"And what are you laughing at?" I grunted.

"The grape does not fall far from the vine," he replied.

I scratched my head. Xerxes was always talking in riddles.

Uncle Zeno smiled. "I think what our Persian friend means is that the odd bit of thievery is part of – what shall I call it? – our family tradition."

This I understood. Uncle Zeno could sell anything. But it wasn't always clear where his "stock" had come from. He would often disappear in the middle of the night – and a whole new range of goods would appear on the stall in the morning.

Today it was mostly leather stuff. And a few pieces of cheap jewellery.

Just then, the crowd started buzzing and Gad the Grump came our way again with an important-looking man and his family.

I heard someone at the next stall say "Jairus", but it didn't mean anything to me. What I did notice was the man's daughter. Jews and Greeks don't usually get along, so I thought she'd ignore me. But she didn't. She smiled!

"Don't pay him any attention," I heard the Grump say. "The boy's not quite right in the head."

Big fat liar. So I smiled back extra hard, just to annoy him.

"He's right, you know," said Uncle Zeno. "You're not right in the head. Not if you fancy that Jewish girl."

"Icch," I said, annoyed and embarrassed all at the same time. "I don't fancy her. She just seems nice. That's all."

"Well, that's a good thing," he nodded. "You see, Greek boys can only marry Jewish girls if they become Jews, too."

"So?" I grunted.

"So," he chuckled again, "that means you'd have to give up those pork sausages you like so much."

"Really?"

"Anyway,"

he continued, "you're far too young to be thinking of girls. What are you, eight?"

"I'm not thinking of girls!" I insisted.

"And he's ten," added Xerxes. "We've had him eight years. He was two when he came to us. Try to keep up."

"A slave who can add," sneered Uncle Zeno. "What a marvellous asset! I don't know what I'd do without you."

"I know," Xerxes muttered again. "The word 'disaster' comes to mind."

"Oh, that's right," Uncle Zeno replied. "Like the disastrous deal I made for you. What did I give? A couple of blankets and three mangy cats. How I miss them now!"

They were like an old married couple, those two. Always fighting. Always making up. But I was tired of the argument, so I interrupted, saying, "Do Jews really not eat pork then? Not at all?"

"My dear Hector," sighed Uncle Zeno, "people do the most ridiculous things in the name of their gods."

"Here we go," sighed Xerxes, rolling his eyes.

"Yes. Yes," Uncle Zeno sighed back. "I know it drives you crazy. But the boy must be taught. Warned against the nonsense that is at the heart of every religion."

"In your opinion," muttered Xerxes.

"In my opinion?" Uncle Zeno repeated in

exasperation. "This from a man who worships Mithra and believes that every living thing sprouted from the bowels of a cow!"

"The belly of a bull," Xerxes answered, wearily.

"Oh yes, that's much more sensible!" Uncle Zeno replied.

"Well, it's as sensible as what you Greeks believe," said Xerxes.

"Not this Greek," Uncle Zeno insisted. "The less intelligent among my people may still believe that Hermes and Zeus wander down to earth and play tricks on us mere mortals. But anyone with half a brain knows that those are just stories – meant to frighten or entertain or control."

And then he looked me straight in the eye. "The reality, my boy, is that there are no gods. There's no heaven up there. And nothing but earth beneath our feet. We're born. We live. We die. That's the end of it. And in the meantime," he winked as a customer cast his eye on a piece of jewellery, "we try to make just as much money as we can!"

Making money was my hope a couple of days later as I sneaked up to the Grump's stall. Uncle Zeno always said that it wasn't how much you could sell something for that counted. It was how much you had to pay for it in the first place. So I thought that if I could steal a few bits from Gad's stall, then whatever I sold them for would be profit!

I waited until there was a crowd. I waited until he was looking the other way.

Or so I thought. Because just as I grabbed for a particularly shiny trinket, a fat hand grabbed my wrist.

"Gotcha!" he sneered. And there's no telling what he would have done had some lady not rushed up to him in a panic.

"Have you heard?" she cried. "Jairus' daughter. She's dying!"

Shocked, he released his grip and I pulled free. But I did not run. "Jairus?" I asked. "The one who was with his daughter the other day?"

"Of course, you imbecile!" the Grump shouted. "She's his only child!"

"He's gone to the centre of town," the lady continued, "to ask Jesus to heal her."

And then the Grump just forgot about me. He picked himself up off his stool and lumbered after the lady.

And, keeping my distance, I followed them.

I know what Uncle Zeno would have said: "Gods. Healing power. Stupid."

But she'd smiled at me. And I guess I just hoped that somehow somebody could make her well. And that didn't seem stupid at all.

When we caught up with Jairus, there were loads of people around him, all hurrying… somewhere.

"Where are we going?" I asked.

"To Jairus' house," someone answered. "But they're saying it's too late."

And sure enough, when the crowd stopped at a big house, someone came rushing forward to meet Jairus. And when he had spoken, Jairus tore his robes and fell to the ground.

Everybody around me started shaking their heads and crying. And then, from the front of the crowd, I heard people laughing! Not nice laughing, though. Sneering, Grump-laughing.

I crept through the crowd. And that's when I found out what the laughing was about.

"Jesus says she's only sleeping," someone sniggered.

"Some prophet he turned out to be," joked someone else.

"The mourners are here, for heaven's sake," sighed another voice. "The girl's dead!"

Uncle Zeno would have had a thing or two to add to that conversation. But I was really sad. The girl was dead. And I'd never even said "hi" to her.

So I pushed my way out of the crowd and wandered around the back side of the house, kicking stones and thinking about what Uncle Zeno had said. How we're born and we live and we die – and that's that. And how it didn't seem fair, somehow, that she'd only lived for a little while.

And then I heard something – something from the top of the house. I stepped back to get a better view and just managed to see the head of somebody in the window. It was Jairus. And standing next to him was another man – who I guessed was the Jesus everyone had been laughing about.

He was smiling, which seemed strange. And then his head disappeared, as if he was bending down. And the next thing I knew, there was another head in the window. The girl. Alive. With her arms wrapped around her father's neck! And he was crying. And she was crying. And I think I was crying, too.

She looked out the window. She looked right at me. And I wiped my eyes with the back of my hand and I waved.

And she waved back.

And then I ran. I don't know why. Maybe because I didn't want her to see me crying. Or because I just didn't know what else to do.

But Uncle Zeno knew. Or at least he had a theory, once I'd told him what had happened.

"It's very clear to me," he grinned. "You ran, my boy, because you suddenly remembered that doing anything else could be very bad news for your pork intake."

I didn't think that was the case, but I laughed anyway. And Xerxes laughed, too. And then he looked very seriously at Uncle Zeno and asked, "Do you doubt the power of God now?"

And Uncle Zeno just kept grinning. "I have no doubts," he began. "No doubts that this Jesus made a very lucky guess. The girl was obviously just sleeping. And he woke her up. Doesn't take a god to do that."

But I wasn't so sure.

"Maybe not," I thought. "But maybe… just maybe… well." It didn't seem like the right time to get into it.

And besides, Gad the Grump would still be on the other side of town. Which meant that it was the perfect time to help myself to a little more of his merchandise!

The Fussy Eater's Version

The Feeding of the Five Thousand

Samuel looked in his basket and sighed. Bread. Lots of bread. But no butter. And no jam.

And fish. Two fish. Flat and salted and hard.

Samuel was no fan of fish. And bread? Bread was not much better. But it was all his mum had packed.

So when lunchtime arrived, Samuel decided he would swap. First he went to his cousin, Anna. "I've got something amazing for my lunch!" he boasted, the basket behind his back. "Wanna swap?"

Anna rolled her eyes. "It's bread and fish, isn't it?" she said.

"Might be," Samuel answered.

"It's what your mum always gives you!" she replied. "You can't fool me. And no, I don't want to swap, because I didn't even bring lunch. My dad thought we'd be home by now."

"Oh," Samuel shrugged. "All right then, I'll ask someone else…

"Someone who doesn't know my mum," he promised himself. "Someone who doesn't know what's in my basket."

So off he went across the hillside, looking for a likely swapper.

He spotted his friend, Micah, but Micah's mum was the worst cook in their village. He'd gone to Micah's house for dinner once, and Micah's mum had served them this soup with bits of stuff floating in it. He thought it was chicken or maybe some kind of overcooked vegetable. But it wasn't. It was brain! Calf brain!

Samuel shuddered. He might not fancy fish. He might be tired of plain old ordinary bread. But there was no way he was going to trade it for a basket of brains!

Micah waved. Samuel waved back. Then he turned as quickly as he could and hurried off in the opposite direction.

"There has to be somebody with a better lunch than mine," he thought. And then he saw another boy from the village, Aaron.

Samuel didn't know Aaron all that well, but he'd heard that Aaron's mum was an amazing cook. It seemed like a good choice.

"Hey, Aaron!" he shouted, the basket behind his back again. "Want to swap lunches?"

Aaron, who was a bit older than Samuel and a great deal taller, folded his arms and looked down at him. "Well," he began, "you know that my mother is the finest cook in the village."

"Yeah, I heard that," Samuel nodded.

"Why, I remember the time we had the mayor over for a meal. Have you met the mayor?" Aaron asked.

"Yeah. Sure," replied Samuel. "Well, we haven't had him over to dinner, but –"

"I didn't think so," Aaron sighed, as if he was already bored with the conversation. But then he went on… "My mother prepared a lovely bit of lamb, marinated in red wine and her own special mixture of herbs…"

And on… "With barley bread… her own unique recipe…"

And on… "And at the end we had some beautiful fresh figs drizzled with honey…"

Samuel tried to get a word in, but it was hopeless. And he found himself in the strangest position – his mouth drooling, his brain turning to mush, and his

feet desperate to carry him as far away as possible.

At last, he just swung the basket in front of Aaron and shouted, "Do you want to swap or not?"

Aaron peeped into the basket and turned up his nose. "You are joking, I hope? That food's not fit for human consumption!"

Samuel shouted again. "It's not drizzled with barley and fresh figs, if that's what you mean!" And he let his feet win the argument and take him to the other side of the hill.

"There must be somebody with something to swap," he muttered to nobody in particular.

But there wasn't. People were talking. People were moving about. Some of them were complaining. But nobody seemed to be eating.

So Samuel resigned himself to his fate, sat himself

down, and reached into his basket.

Just then, someone sat down beside him. It was someone he didn't know. A young man, maybe eighteen or nineteen years old.

"My name's Andrew," said the man.

Samuel slowly withdrew his hand from the basket. "You don't want to swap, by any chance, do you?" he asked.

"Swap?" replied Andrew, surprised. "No. No. I don't have anything to swap with you!"

Samuel rolled his eyes. Another lost cause.

"What I did wonder, though – and this is going

to sound strange," Andrew went on, "was if you wouldn't mind coming with me and showing your lunch to Jesus?"

"Jesus?" Samuel shrugged. "The guy who's been doing all the talking?"

"Teaching. Yeah," Andrew nodded. "He's a rabbi – and that's what he does."

"And now he wants my lunch?"

"I told you it would sound strange," said Andrew. "Look, here he is. Jesus! Here's a boy. A boy with something to eat."

Jesus joined them. "Excellent!" he grinned. And then he turned to Samuel. "Would you mind," he asked, "if I borrowed your lunch for a bit?"

This was getting stranger still. And Samuel didn't mind saying so. "How do you borrow somebody's lunch?" he asked.

"Hand me the basket," Jesus smiled, "and I'll show you!"

Jesus shut his eyes and bowed his head. So did Andrew. And Samuel joined in – it seemed the polite thing to do.

Jesus thanked God for the fish. Jesus thanked God for the bread. Samuel was relieved that he didn't have to join in for that bit. He wasn't, to be perfectly honest, feeling very thankful.

And then, when all the thanking was over, Jesus reached into the basket and pulled out a piece of

bread. He broke it in half. He broke it in quarters. But the more he broke it, the more there seemed to be.

Samuel rubbed his eyes. Was this some sort of trick?

But no – the more Jesus broke, the more there was. And it was just the same with the fish.

Andrew and some of Jesus' other friends started passing the fish and bread around, and soon everybody on that hillside was eating fish and bread. Samuel shook his head. There must have been thousands of them!

When Jesus had finished and everyone had been fed, he handed the basket back to Samuel. There were still two fish and five pieces of bread inside.

"That's how you borrow somebody's lunch," Jesus whispered. "Thanks for playing along."

Samuel stood up slowly and staggered away, shocked and amazed by what he'd seen. So shocked, in fact, that he failed to watch where he was going and bumped straight into Aaron.

"Watch it!" Aaron grunted. And then he added, "Oh, it's you. Still carrying around that pathetic excuse for a lunch, are you? Well, I'll have you know that I have just had the most incredible meal. Fish and bread like you've never tasted. I'm dying to tell Mother about it."

And he rushed away.

Samuel thought about saying something. But what was the point? Aaron would never have believed it anyway.

"On the other hand," he thought, "if snooty Aaron thinks it's so great…"

And he tore off a piece of bread. And he took a bite of a piece of fish. And then he smiled at the miracle in his mouth.

For… it… was… delicious!

The Boring Version

Jesus and the Little Children

Nathan hated waiting. "It's hot," he moaned. "I'm bored," he groaned. "What are we doing here anyway?"

"If I have told you once," sighed his mum, "I have told you a hundred times. We are waiting to see Rabbi Jesus, so that he can ask for God's blessing on you."

"But I don't want to be blessed!" Nathan sighed back. "I want to go and play with my friends."

"That's the strangest thing I ever heard," grunted Aunt Rebecca, who was waiting with her twins right behind him. "Not wanting to be blessed!"

"So do you two want to be blessed?" Nathan asked the twins.

"Pickle," said Moses.

"Poo," giggled Jake.

"I'm taking that as a 'no'," said Nathan.

"They are two years old!" huffed Aunt Rebecca. "You can hardly expect them to understand."

"Well, I'm ten and I don't understand either," Nathan grumbled. "I mean, what good is it, being blessed? Does it make you cleverer? Does it make you happier? Does it make you richer?"

"It doesn't make you anything," his mum answered. "It's just a way of asking God to be with you – to take care of you. What's wrong with that?"

"Nothing, I guess," Nathan shrugged. "If it doesn't take all day!"

"We've only been here for an hour," sighed Aunt Rebecca. "That's hardly all day."

"Ducky," added Moses.

"Poo," giggled Jake.

Another hour went by, and Nathan spent most of that time on the ground, cracking one rock against another.

"We haven't even moved," he moaned. "There's nothing to do," he groaned. "Why is this taking so long?"

"It's kind of hard to tell," said Nathan's mum,

standing on her tiptoes and craning her neck to see ahead. "There are a lot of ill people who come to see Jesus to be healed. Perhaps that's why it's taking so long."

"You'd think he'd do all the quick stuff first," Nathan grumbled. "A blessing here. A blessing there. Get it out of the way. And then get on with the harder things."

"I'm sure it doesn't work that way," huffed Aunt Rebecca.

"How do you know?" asked Nathan. "Have you ever seen Jesus heal anybody?"

"Well… no… not personally," she was huffing again. And puffing a bit, too. "But I just know – we have to take our turn. And you have to be a little more patient!"

"I've been very patient!"

Nathan cried. "We've been here for two hours!"

"And we'll stay here until we see him!" she insisted. "You should take a lesson from the twins. They're not complaining."

Nathan rolled his eyes. "They're asleep!"

"Snn-rrr-fff," snuffled Moses.

"Poozzzzzz," snored Jake.

Another hour passed and still there was no movement.

Nathan lay on his back, perfectly still, staring into the sky.

"Get up!" grunted Aunt Rebecca. "You're embarrassing us!"

"But I'm paralysed," said Nathan through clenched teeth. "Can't you see I need help? Maybe someone will notice and they'll let us jump the queue."

"I'll do something if you don't get up!" his aunt threatened. "And then you really will need help."

"Mum!" cried Nathan, teeth still clenched. "Aunt Rebecca is being particularly hateful to a poor paralysed person who only wants a bit of a blessing and a miracle or two."

"It's not funny, Nathan," his mum sighed. "And it's nothing to joke about. Get up."

"All right," he moaned, sitting up. "Hey, look, I'm healed!"

"Very amusing," huffed Aunt Rebecca.

Moses sat there quietly.

But Jake had lots to say. "Poo", mostly. And "Poo".

Sometime in the middle of hour number four, the queue began to move.

"At last!" shouted Nathan. "We get blessed and then we go home! Finally!"

"That's what it looks like," said his mum, craning her neck again. "Jesus' helpers seem to be making two queues. One for people who have children. And one for those who don't."

"What did I tell you?" Nathan grinned. "They're gonna do us first and then get on with the hard cases. One of those helpers must have been listening to me."

Aunt Rebecca shook her head. "You really do have a high opinion of yourself, don't you, young man? As if Jesus' helpers would take advice from you! Why, that's just a load of…"

"Puppies," said Moses.

And Jake? Jake was nowhere to be found.

"Where did he go?" cried Aunt Rebecca. "He was here – I saw him just a minute ago!"

"Don't worry, Aunt!" Nathan replied. "He can't have gone far. I'll find him."

And off he disappeared into the crowd.

Nathan ducked and squirmed and wriggled through a maze of feet and legs and children. Lots of them looked like Jake from behind. But Nathan would not be fooled. And finally, he found his cousin right at the front.

"There you are!" he shouted.

And he was immediately shushed.

"Quiet!" said one of the waiting parents. "Jesus' helpers are about to tell us what to do."

"Go home." That's the first thing that Jesus' helpers said. And the second thing was even worse. "Jesus has more important things to do. He doesn't have time for all these children."

Everyone was shocked. And stunned into silence. Everyone but Nathan.

"Go home?" he shouted. "GO HOME?? We've been standing in this queue for hours, bored out of our minds, waiting for just one little blessing. I'm not even sure what a blessing is, but I have waited and waited and waited for one and I am not going home until I get it!"

"Nathan!" called his mother, bursting through the crowd. "Nathan, it's not your place to speak. Be quiet!"

"That's right!" added Aunt Rebecca. "BE QUIET!" And then she looked around the angry crowd.

"He's not MY son, mind you," she added.

"But he's right!" someone shouted.

"It's not him we're angry at!" shouted someone else.

"It's them!" shouted several people at once. And they were pointing at Jesus' helpers.

"And so you should be," came another

voice. Jesus' voice. And it was angry, too.

"I don't know what you were thinking!" he said to his helpers. And he picked up Jake and handed him to one of them. "Children are trusting and loving and innocent. They are exactly the kind of people I want in the new world I'm making. In fact, if you want to follow me, you need to become just like them – not chase them away. Let the children come to me, that's what I say."

And the crowd gave a cheer.

Then Jesus put his hand on Nathan's head and prayed for him.

"Thanks," Nathan smiled. "I'm still not sure what a blessing is, but I'm glad you gave me one. And I'm even more glad that you told off those helpers of yours. The one holding Jake in his arms looks as if he really learned his lesson."

"He does look upset," Jesus nodded.

"And maybe just a little disgusted," observed Nathan's mum.

"Oh yeah, can you smell…?" added Nathan.

And that's when Aunt Rebecca cringed and cried, "Jakey, no!"

And Jake? Jake just giggled.

"Poo."

The Biting Version

Zacchaeus the Tax Collector

"Life is full of surprises." That's what my dad always says. "You can never really tell what's going to happen next."

So there we were, waiting on the side of the street. Stacked up, five-deep. Me and my brother Isaac and just about everybody else in Jericho.

I couldn't see a thing, to be honest. Abraham, the fattest man in town, stood right in front of me. And the fact that he was a fishmonger meant that he was also the smelliest man in town. It was not a good combination.

"Let's move," I whispered to Isaac. And then somebody bumped up behind us. I say "bumped". It was more like a push, like a shove. So I turned around to shout, "Hey, watch it!" or something like that. And – surprise! – I found myself face to face with one mean, scary little man. And I do mean "little". I'm only twelve, and I had a good five centimetres on him.

He didn't say a word. He just scowled and backed up out of the crowd and disappeared somewhere down the queue.

"You know who that is, don't you?" Isaac asked. "That's Zacchaeus, the tax collector."

"Are you sure?" I said.

"Positive," he nodded. "I was in the shop when he came around that time…"

"Oh yeah, that time," I nodded in reply. "The time his bully boys beat Dad senseless."

"I was hiding in the corner behind the big pots," Isaac remembered. "Dad kept saying that he'd paid his taxes already. And they kept saying that there had been a – what did they call it? – 'clerical error', and that he owed them even more."

"Rubbish!" I grumbled. "They just wanted more – and they reckoned they could scare him into handing it over."

"Well, he didn't," Isaac said. "He told them he'd paid what he owed and that was that. And that's

when they smashed things up. The pots, the bowls, and then Dad.

"And Zacchaeus – he didn't say a word. He just stood there with his arms folded, blank-faced, as if it didn't bother him at all. As if he'd seen it a million times before."

"I hate that guy!" I said.

"I hate him, too," Isaac agreed.

"So why don't we do something about it?" I suggested.

"Are you joking?" Isaac snorted. "His goons will have us for dinner."

"I didn't see any goons," I shrugged. "I think he was on his own."

"Now that you mention it," Isaac nodded, "neither did I. If they'd been there, they would have done the pushing and the shoving for him. He'd be standing at the front right now, with the best view in town."

"Which is also kind of weird," I said. "I mean, everybody is waiting for Jesus to arrive. Why would somebody like Zacchaeus even want to see Jesus?"

"Who knows?" Isaac replied. "Maybe rabbis pay taxes, too. Let's go!"

So we wriggled our way out of the crowd and ran down the back of the queue in the same direction the tax collector had gone, stopping every second or two to look for him.

We searched for what seemed like ages. The queue was huge. But then Isaac spotted him right at the end. And that's when it occurred to me that we might not be the only people in that crowd who would like to get their hands on Zacchaeus.

So I ducked back into the crowd, where the mean little crook couldn't see me, and jumped up and down, shouting, "Zacchaeus is here! Zacchaeus the tax collector. He's down at the end of the queue!"

"What?" grunted the man next to me.

"Sorry?" said another man. "What are you going on about, boy?"

"Zacchaeus! The tax collector! He's just down there. And he hasn't got his bodyguards with him!"

"Yeah, right," the first man scoffed. "He doesn't

go anywhere without his bodyguards."

"And what would he be doing here anyway?" added the second man. "Zacchaeus wouldn't be interested in anything Jesus had to say. And you can bet that Jesus wouldn't want to have anything to do with him!"

I was getting nowhere with those guys, so I popped back out of the crowd again, and there he was. Zacchaeus had his back to me and was heading for a tree. A sycamore tree, right where the queue of people ended. He was moving pretty fast. I wasn't really sure what I'd do if I caught him anyway. And then the strangest thing happened. Zacchaeus started climbing up the tree – like some evil, tax-collecting monkey. Surprise!

"Did you see that?" Isaac shouted, running back to meet me.

"Yeah," I sighed. "Now that he's up in that tree, there's no way anybody's going to get their hands on him."

"We'll just have to make sure he can't come down," Isaac grinned. "We'll make sure he stays there until the crowd thins out."

"And how are we going to do that?" I asked.

And Isaac just whistled.

"Bite!" I shouted. "Bite! Good boy! Where did you come from?"

"When I was looking for the tax collector," Isaac

explained, "I ran into Uncle Simon. He had Bite
with him and I told him I'd watch him for a bit.
I reckoned he would come in handy."

"And he has!" I smiled.

Bite was not the biggest dog in town. Not by a long shot. In fact, he was sort of a doggy version of Zacchaeus. Little and mean and horrible.

"If we stand at the bottom of the tree," I suggested, "and let Bite do his thing, I'm pretty sure we can keep the monkey-man up there until someone realizes where he is."

So we wandered over to the tree. Bite barked and snarled and leaped up against the trunk for all he was worth. It was perfect!

Then somebody shouted, "Jesus is coming!" and the crowd roared.

Some people were just cheering, but a lot of them were asking him to come to dinner, too. It was a real honour to have somebody famous eat at your house. I guessed he'd probably end up with the mayor or maybe one of the leaders at the synagogue.

I kept one eye on the crowd and one eye on Jesus, and Bite kept both eyes on the evil monkey-man in the tree. A closer look at Jesus, however, revealed that he was staring at the tree as well.

"Hello, Zacchaeus," he said.

And the crowd started buzzing. "Zacchaeus?"

"Zacchaeus!"

"What's he doing here?"

But the buzzing turned to a dead and stony silence (and even Bite stopped barking!) when Jesus spoke again. "I'm looking for a place to eat," he continued.

"I was thinking that your house might do."

The silence didn't last long. There was moaning and complaining and more swearing than I thought I'd ever hear at a "religious" event.

"It's an outrage!"

"Has Jesus gone mad?"

"Zacchaeus is the worst sinner in town!" the crowd howled.

And Bite howled, too. Until Uncle Simon appeared and dragged him away, embarrassed.

And Jesus? Jesus waited for the tax collector to climb down. Then he followed him home with half the crowd in tow, angry still, but also curious to see what would happen.

"So much for that plan," Isaac sighed.

"Yeah, it doesn't seem right. He beats up our dad, then he gets to eat with the most important visitor this town has ever had. I thought Jesus was a good guy."

"Maybe he has a dog, too," Isaac chuckled. "Hidden under those robes of his."

"That would be a surprise!" I grinned. "But I sort of doubt it. I wouldn't mind seeing what happens now. The crowd's pretty worked up. Let's watch."

So off we went. And then we waited. It took ages. But finally, Zacchaeus' front door opened, and he and Jesus came out (to more than a few boos).

"I have an announcement to make!" Zacchaeus shouted. "I have decided to give half of what I own to the poor."

That shut the crowd up.

"Furthermore, if I have cheated any of you, I will pay you back four times what I took."

Silence. Shock. And then the biggest cheer I have

ever heard. And then Jesus spoke. "Salvation has come to this house today," he said. "And that is why I have come – to seek out and to save those who are lost."

There was another cheer, and then Zacchaeus began walking toward my brother and me. Had he seen us with Bite? Did he suspect anything? Would Jesus step in and save us, too?

"You're the potter's boys, aren't you?" he said.

"That's right," I answered nervously.

"That's us," added Isaac.

"Well, I cannot tell you how sorry I am for what happened to your father," he continued. "Or rather," correcting himself, "what I did to your father."

Then he held out a moneybag, and I swear I saw tears in his eyes.

"Please take this to him," he said, "with my most humble apologies and my assurances that nothing like that will ever happen again."

He put the bag in my hand, wiped his eyes, and then walked away.

"I didn't expect that," Isaac whispered.

"Me neither," I whispered back.

It's like my dad always says, I guess. Life is full of surprises.

Also by Bob Hartman

Bible Baddies
More Bible Baddies
Stories from the Stable
The Lion Storyteller Easter Book
Old Testament Tales: The Unauthorized Version